PERENNIAL WISDOM

A TREASURE TROVE OF SHORT STORIES AND POEMS

DR. ALOK CHANDRA AND
DR. MUKTA GOYAL

Contents

Contents

Foreword

It gives me indeed great joy to write the foreword for the present anthology entitled ***"Perennial Wisdom:A Treasure Trove of Short Stories and Poems"*** Edited by Dr Alok Chandra and Dr Mukta Goyal. This is really a wonderful collection of remarkable creative writings of a bunch of contributors from pan India with rich fragrance of wisdom. I am so very excited to see the original creative works of literature with superior quality. It stands evident for the real hard work of both the editors.

The short stories are very much interesting and give rewarding experience throughout the same would be experienced by all the readers of this anthology for sure. The poems are soulful in nature and take us to the next level of understanding the self, society, nature and life.

It's is yet another jewel in the crown of literary world in terms of varied spheres of knowledge and wisdom.

The contributors of this beautiful anthology have tried to shake the world gently through their creative writings of poems and short stories. I am extremely confident and hopeful that the readers of this anthology would get immensely benefitted by reading these pieces of literature which in turn would make them as enlightened human beings of wisdom. Literature always makes the life more meaningful, especially the poems and short stories would make the humans more gentle and refined in nature.

This kind of literary venture is the need of the hour, especially when the whole human race is reeling under catastrophic condition of helplessness and uncertainty due to pandemic.

I extend my sincere wishes and appreciations to all the contributors and the editors of this anthology for their selfless duty towards helping the humanity by installing the hope and positivity in the minds of the readers through their creative work.

May the whole world enjoy happiness, prosperity, wisdom and peace.

Dr Saravanan V

Assistant Professor Senior

Department of English,

School of Social Sciences and Languages,

Vellore Institute of Technology, (VIT) Vellore-632 014 Tamil Nadu, India.

Preface

The present anthology entitled *"Perennial Wisdom: A Treasure Trove of Short Stories and Poems"* contains precious gems in the form of captivating stories and poems. It is drenched in the elixir of manifold wisdom and the same is the outcome of the contributors' strong passion as well as unbreakable commitment to make the present anthology an effective means of social and ecological awareness. It mirrors the creative writers' real literary calibre or talents who have gifted the present literary work a bunch of relevant themes.

Moreover, the most striking feature of this anthology is grounded on the concrete facts of its perennial usefulness as well as wisdom which bestow elevated eyesight to worldly people ensuring their heartiest, respect, love, sympathy, care, etc, towards both the domestic and the natural creatures or objects of the blue planet.

In addition to this, the entire creative writings (both short stories and poems) work as a pool to make both humans and components of nature connect with one other in terms of the holistic idea of Vasudev Kutumabkam.

It is quite certain that any reader will gain evergreen wisdom or skill in the creative writings after plunging into the oceanic world of the present anthology consisting of the finest short stories and poems.

Moreover, it plays an everlasting role as a guide to making the worldly people get rid of the insensible thoughts of bias, discrimination, jealousy, enmity, etc.

I extend my heartiest gratitude to all the short story writers and poets for their timely contributions in bringing their works in the form of an edited anthology.

I am happy to say that the entire contents of this published work are the best outcomes of my contributors' strong literary potential and will prove decisive in terms of making the readers cultivate and cherish the sublime thoughts of kinship, honesty, integrity, etc.

Dr. Alok Chandra

Dr. Mukta Goyal

List Of Short Stories And Poems

List Of Authors

1. **Disha Madan**
2. **P. V. B.Sriramamurthy**
3. **Dr. Alok Chandra**
4. **Bhallam Anil Raju**
5. **Dr. Rachna Rastogi**
6. **Dr. Mukta Goyal**
7. **Dr. Jaya Ghosh**
8. **Dr. Jyoti Patil**
9. **Dr. Devimeenakshi. K**
10. **Arundhati Dutta Choudhury**
11. **Rayba Saindane**
12. **Semanti Kumar**
13. **Aashi**
14. **Chethna Vivek N**
15. **Nafisa Jhosawa**
16. **Tenzin Tsetan**
17. **Venkatesan Sai Taruni**
18. **Shrishti Kothari**

1. From Darkness to Light

****Disha Madan***

Far away, in the woods, lived a lonely figure called Bob. A strong and sturdy personality, an architect by profession, he was profusely called a builder. A poet at heart, living lavishly in passion, thought of life as a short journey, bedecked with thorns and roses. This universe seemed to him as replete with silent voices to be heard in seclusion. Reflecting on the foregone days, he smiled and thought that expertise comes with maturity. Each drop of the ocean contributes in its own manner to form the body of its complete and enormous self. Disturbance in a single drop causes turbulence in the whole part. Bit by bit, step by step, life partakes as a battlefield. Each breath pushes the life a step behind, moving forward towards an end, which is in fact the beginning.

Bob had lived in a society where health, wealth, and affluence shined in the lives of the people. Fun and frolic were the order of the day. Of course, he had to run hither and thither to meet the two ends of his life. But, he was never afraid of hard work. With talent proficiency and a spark in him, he reached the heights too soon. During this journey, he stumbled upon so many lives, tarried with different personalities, and resided with faith and inspiration.

Bob had come across many people and he had been hurt any number of times. When hurts and pains wound the heart, the threshed yarns of the heart keep peeping out of the lacerated body. A wounded heart pains and reacts with third-degree pains. The cauldron of fire burning in the heart requires endless ounces of cool waters to calm it down. Hot blood flows in his arteries and veins which is always ready to erupt anytime. The moment the temperature of the body increases, the heart gives way to innumerable passionate attacks. Wonderstruck, Bob gazes on in the blank life ahead.

A pure and innocent heart that wants to lead a true life is always struck and jarred by a merciless world. If a pure heart wants to lead a simple life, innumerable obstructions mash the heart and leave the heart bleeding, which in turn feels immensely weak. The weak heart is set ablaze. The heart and the oozing blood, together, enmesh the body. The pure heart shouldn't be weak enough to give in. But, the beatings received at regular intervals leave no space for breath. Strangled, the heart gives in to await a new birth with a new conscious.

The ups and downs of life, at times, pass on a certain kind of strength. The visibility of the strength gives a genuine cause to survive. The spark within oneself keeps the self on the move. An amalgamation of yellow, green, peach, and saffron make the walk soothing and peaceful. The burning heart breathes in this white, peaceful breeze. The aura of unachieved dreams bounces against the huge black wall, wondering.... Is there no end to this painstaking life ???

Bob's mind when sets to ponder over the peculiarity of life, it's difficult for him to pull himself out of the bygone times. As the present has its roots in the past, hence, to completely cut off oneself from it is not possible. Yet, the process of life proceeds despite one's knowledge. Leading a solitary life was never easy for him. He recalled the days, months, years he had spent with his loved one. Thinking so, his eyes gushed with tears rolling down his cheeks in a row like incessant drizzling. This drizzle turned into hauling cries without his mind's permission. His heart throbbed recurrently questioning how far he was responsible for his situation today. The arrows of innumerable questions seeped through his heart. Certain questions do not hold legitimate answers.

Bob was happily married to a beautiful girl called Zora. There was no answer as to why he married her. He fell in love with her the very first time he saw her. Love, at first sight, did fetch miracles. She also submitted herself unto him. This nuptial was rather a quick process. They both lived happily and merrily. The air of passion and love permeated their lives. Sorrow was miles away from them. Both shared similar habits to a certain extent. Hither and thither, a habit which created certain difference was silently shoved to a corner. A corner which was to pile up bit by bit to form a mountain.

Happiness comes from within. They together created smiles, spread joy and happiness. One can distribute a thing to the world which one possesses. The aura of laughter and goodness bloomed in their garden, their neighbors, and the little world which surrounded them. Their home was bedecked with roses and pearls.

In the morning, Zora would wake up Bob with zestful eyes. A touch of spirituality spread through her which surfaced her body in the mornings. The earnestness with which she offered prayers was really laudable. The space around her would always be replete with purity and freshness. With such feelings dwelling in her heart, she would wake up Bob silently. It used to be like a silent wake-up call that travelled through the materialistic body. It would breathe freshness into the lazy and lethargic sleeping guy. Such was her first contact with her other half. She wanted to restore courage in him and throw out desperate thoughts from his restless mind. Everyone possesses the spark to survive encouragingly. But, to keep the spark glowing is another process through which the journey of life persists.

Bob, on the other hand, would wake up with a flash. Being on the receiving end, his inner spark would immediately respond. He would hug her and get up to tarry through life with infinite fervor and willpower. He responded with strong willpower to face the world with determination. As the foundation of one's life is laid deep during the formative years, so does the music of the heart grows and responds along with its roots. Then the body and the soul frolic with deep-seated happiness. Thus, was the state of two hearts mingled into one.

Bob, the architect, labored hard to meet the two ends of life. No matter what dangers life brings in one's life, they seem petty when the heart has all the courage to go through it coolly. Life pushed Bob to work hard for the sake of Zora. His evenings with her were not bereft of passion and love. A soul thus tarrying rejoices in a joint venture of body and soul. The strings of destiny keep on playing the music while the human being dances to its tune.

Zora's inner spark turned the pages of spirituality a bit too fast. Too rapid was the pace for Bob to digest. The intake was more and the digestion was slow. This imbalance started injecting an incurable illness. The speed of the intake of her breath was pretty fast. The input was more than the output. This imbalance in Zora's self-started caused a little uneasiness in her fabulous life.

Zora started worshipping her Lord with a spectacular speed. Gradually, she took to religious hymns. Her mind and heart took a steep turn from Bob's heart to the Maker of the Universe. The smiles shared with Bob sounded fake to her. She felt the need to look into the principles of birth and death. From where did the man come and where he was heading towards…amidst these quests she was losing herself. Sages and saints have wondered years together in search of these answers. The paucity of knowledge and devotion leaves one to a certain level of negativity. A strain of optimism is the prerequisite of sublimity. Zora was lost in search of queries of life.

Bob, in turn, was always trying to convince Zora's shooting emotions. At times, he was successful in convincing her, but, most of the time he failed. As, life's queries do not find answers easily, life itself proves to be a big riddle with deeply embedded answers. But, there is an obstacle – a stone- in the throat which makes it a formidable task to form a spiritual link. This happens when communication between the Super Soul and the soul wriggles to materialize. This ecstatic sublime intercom forwards the journey of the soul back to its own permanent Home.

The fractured souls are wondering helter-skelter trying to rectify the incessant rotation of birth and death. Even a little effort by the human being to cross the ocean of materialism pushes him a step ahead of the common mob. But, the human beings is engrossed in the race of materialism. He is stuck badly in the marshy outlet. Though he is aware of the path, but is, at times, unable to cross the ocean. As his feet are screwed to the marshy earth surrounded by spikes. A genius or a blessed fortunate chosen one is able to help himself out of the row and is able to cross the ocean. The dilemma of life is, whilst, one makes an effort to swim across, the people gathered around the glue and entice one to the ground strongly.

But, Zora's spark was becoming a big and bright star. The light inside her was spreading amazingly. She was gifted to spread goodness within herself and the people around her. Hither and thither, Bob gulped down this fact of life. He accepted the hard truth that she was just not made only for him. She was made to spread the light in the universe. It took him many disturbed nights to reach this conclusion. Days and nights of struggle in the mind and heart had turned him into a stone. It was an enormous lapse in his life that heralded no chemical, medicinal cure. How long could he behold her in his arms? His life was entrapped in a mess that had no remedy. All the money together in this world could not buy happiness for him. He had never ever surmised of such a vacant life.

Zora wanted to leave for good. The call had come. Now, no one could stop her. When the call comes, it is so strong, that the near and dear ones' efforts to behold the person go in vain. It was no use stopping her. Bob did not move while he sat through the last night with her. She had announced to leave the following dawn. She was going to join the church, the Holy Communion, and would soon lead a life of a nun. Bob's face was white with fear, sadness, helplessness, and whatnot. He was at such a drastic turn of his life that he could not love his own betrothed wife. He sat pondering…is this the same Zora whom he loves incessantly and she too in turn surrendered completely unto him ??? There was not an inkling of doubt about there being infinite lovers. Since their nuptials, for twenty long years, they resided as two sweet bunnies. Who could doubt a sacrificing, loving husband to be so strong in love even after twenty long years of togetherness? She had never been in favor of giving birth to children. Bob never objected to this decision of hers. He had starkly given his all to her. Was this what he was getting in return? How the time flew, he never knew. Now suddenly, life became a burden for him. Not because of how he would live without Zora, but the thought that what he had earned out of life, disturbed him more and more. Certain figures of life suddenly vanish from the screen. There is no reason – to answer – no option for it.

Bob's heart was becoming cold. His hands and legs went numb. How he wished that morn may never come. He dreamt that moon would stay by for a few more hours. The time to part may never befall on him. But, time never waits. The wheel of time moves on and on. People come and go. Days, nights, months, years pass by but the wheel of time never tires out. It never has mercy. It is like an impartial Supreme judge. Who does not perturb and touch anyone's life, nor is it touched by grief, joy, or sorrow. And, Bob was not an exception. The finale of his so-called joys did arrive. Both parted with a heavy heart and brimming eyes. There is no measuring rod to measure the depth of love. There is just a sensibility, a feeling, of possessing a heart or being sans it. Life moves on and pushes thousands along with it. The dilemma of roughness with smoothness portrays different characters like you and me.

Years passed by. Bob did not marry again. In these ten years, Zora served the soul. It was not only her own soul but whomsoever she came in contact with, their soul was destined to rise. She was at par with a holy saint. On the other hand, Bob still waited for her return. Life was a beautiful tussle between receiving and giving. In this skirmish, the judgment day arrived. The strong bond of love which never fueled away between the two brought them face to face.

Bob was down with fever. There was no one to look after him. Zora looked after the suffering humanity. And, Bob was one of them. She paid a visit to Bob to inquire about him every day. And, one fine day, Bob's call came. He was about to breathe his last. And, Zora was beside his bed. He had wished to die in her arms. And, his wish was fulfilled. And, Zora could not breathe anymore as soon as Bob died. The souls of Bob and Zora rose from darkness to light.

2. Behind Draupadi's Laughter….

*****ORIGINAL: TELUGU WRITTEN By***
[1]P. V. B.SRIRAMAMURTHY
*****TRANSLATED INTO ENGLISH By***
[2]Dr KARUNANIDHI KETIREDDY.

It is Sarat Rithu.

Moon is spilling its light on this earth giving a heavenly splendour. The earth is as if it were floating in the ocean of milk. The mansions in it are like the ships laden with goods carrying them to the far off places. In a skyscraper, seated on the jewel-studded throne, placing her long, black and shining meandering braid in her lap is Draupadi.. the queen of Pandavaas. Flowers set in her hair are shedding their fragrance.

At that juncture, having finished a royal task or activity, entered, Dharma

Raja, Pandavaas' eldest.

" O, Queen! My dear Queen!!" Called he. There is no answer. He searched for her in the mansion, enquired about the servant maids. But couldn't find her.

It is his meeting her, after the lapse of five

Years. It is their first night. How thrilling and eager is his heart to meet her! Anxiously and intently awaiting! Having searched for her downstairs, he has reached upstairs. There are the statues.

The sculpture is exuding.

" Here, you are! " saying so he hugged her behind. Made her breathless with his kisses. Such is her bewitching beauty that even the moon god can't resist himself from kissing her with his light.

Intoxicated is Dharmaraja. Revelling with

Joy is in her presence.

" O my dear queen, may ask you a question? Would you answer truly?

" Ever lied earlier? "

" Never. Know pretty well you never lie.

Let me shoot it. We, the Pandavas, are your five husbands. Are looking after you well each trying to excel the other. Of all, who do you like among us ? " asked Dharmaraja.

To this question, Draupadi laughed. Gone into peels of laughter.

" What has made you laugh? "

" Your question has reminded me Arjuna. "

" Why?"

Again Draupadi laughed. Her laugh echoed in that peaceful light.

As a swear he made to her, he didn't ask that question again.

On that moonlight night immersed has Dharmaraaja been in her moonlight gurgling laugh.

? ? ?

It is Greeshama Ruth.

Peak summer.. Very sultry.

Touching his braid chest is Bheema sitting in udyaanavana or the garden. It has been five years since he is in the presence of Draupadi. As per their agreement, each one of them has to spend a year with Draupadi. Now it's Vaayunandana's turn.

He is now with Draupadi. The rejoining is very exciting and thrilling. Very heartening.

Draupadi has caught hold of his moustache with her teeth.

" When I am in your presence, Draupadi everything else, everyone else seems to be waste or nothing.

" May I ask you a question?"

" Please do, my lord. "

" Must you tell the truth! "

"Have no belief! "

" Why this question? " A lot of belief. Ok. I want to know ...

"Who is your favourite in our Pandavaas.?"

To his query, Draupadi laughed roaringly.

" Why have you laughed? "

" Savyasaachi.. the ambidextrous... has flashed to my mind.

On listening to this, Bheema became silent.

Having said so, she, without wasting, any more time, embraced him. They became absorbed unto each other. Bound by the promise he made to her, he couldn't ask that question.

... .

Nakula is standing before the looking glass. Gold complexion. Fascinating beauty or handsomeness even for men. Hair like that of a Firefly. Lotus-eyed. Broad-shouldered. His sword prowess to cut anything into the minutest possible.

While those thoughts are passing through her mind, Draupadi is looking at him ecstatically. " My beloved queen, why are you staring at me? "

"How have I been severed from your association? " said she with her sleepy eyes.

Uh-huh! Do you like it that much? "

"Should I say it? "

" Bye, the bye, which one of our five brothers are you enamoured of? "

Pat came Draupadhi,' s laugh. Hysterically,

Though!

" Why are you laughing? " asked Nakula being confused.

" Reminded of Arjuna? "

" Reason? "

By just unmindful of his question she

Floated him in her joy world.

Committed to his promise, he didn't ask the question again.

… … …

Taking Sahadeva's fingers as tender as betel leaves into hers, said Draupadi.

" How pretty you are? "

"True? Then who among us has closely come to your heart. " asked Sahadeva. Draupadi laughed as she did in the earlier occasions.

" What has caused you to laugh? "

" Savyasaachi has figured in my mind. "

" what for? "

Shadeva's query shuddered her. It quickened her beat because Sahadeva is astrological expertise in knowing past, present and future. At once she made him promise not to ask that question again.

Without wasting any fraction of time,

Draupadi took him to love the world.

… … …

Dwaithavan.

All the brothers are sitting and exchanging pleasantries. At a point the question of who among them that Draupadhi likes very much surfaced. Undoubtedly,

Arjuna pat came to the answer. Unanimously it has sounded. At that juncture, Draupadi

Us passing that way, Yudhistira called him

And put before her their doubt

Again, She laughed. Her laughter has echoed this entire world.

" Why are you laughing ? " said Bhima angrily and sullenly.

" Cool down. My dear darlings, show me your fingers of both hands.

Good. Now, can you tell me

Which one of these your favourite is. Beauty lies when only all are united. You all should be safe and strong when united. It is safe for me and the world also . " reasoned she. " Not only that. There is a great meaning than this. You are the weapons of Srihari…. The protector. Lord Srirama's five horses. Of you all, it was Arjuna who first shot that question. The chilipidanam prank that sounded in his tone when he put that question to me made me laugh unendingly.

That Paramaathma.. and my brother, on putting my foot here as a daughter-in-law, has cautioned me to look after you all as carefully as my five fingers. I have just done what he told me. Hereafter, there is no room for that question.

" What do you say, darlings. ? "

The Pandavas got an answer to their teasing question. They felt happy.

… … …

Soon after reading the story, Dharitri asked her mother…

" What has prompted you to write this? "

Subhadra began to explain.

What is your understanding of the story? If Draupadi had uttered any one of the Pandavas as her favourite what would have happened? That has led to their division. They would fight with each other. In the process, they get killed. Has it been so, what happens? Evildoers and scamps will rule this world. To prevent that calamity, she has behaved so. How wisely and discreetly! The Pandavas are great warriors. Yet, they are Male. How intelligently she has conducted herself managing all her five husbands.

The next day, Dharitri is on the way to her mother-in-law's house.

3. Friendship: An Inspirational Story of Utmost Determination and Honesty

****Dr. Alok chandra***

The story begins in campus of a renowned college in Rajasthan. The day is very special in the lives of Sangam hostel.

The first ray of the morning not only reminds them about packing their books, shoes, notebooks, keroisine lantern, etc, in their woolen bags but also intensifies their collective hope of meeting their families after a gap of one-year. This day showcases their craziness of leaving the hostel at the earliest.

Tripathi, Sajan, Deepesh and Tinku are very fast friends ; they have maintained their mutual friendship ever since they were allotted to the same room to pursue their B.A. degrees in English literature. They also never loose a single chance of extending their timely thankfulness to one another. All the roommates have a special appreciation for Tripathi for having a special privilege of cooking delicious food dishes but they show their empathy for today's lunch as they have decided to take fruits in order to avoid any delay in reaching the railway station.

Tripathi is not an ordinary soul ; since his childhood days he was habituated to read Swami Vivekananda's holistic ideas through buying booklets which were available in the book shops of the local market adjoining his village.

The village was surrounded with green trees and a small pond, too, enlarged its natural beauty. That is why he, before evacuating his hostel, he goes for making Dahi-bara as relishing this tasty and special dish ensures the safe and fruitful journey to any particular place or destination. Moreover, to taste curd is always conceived of embracing the best luck in humans' earthly lives.

The story now get focused on the entrance door of the hostel as all these friends are saying goodbye to it and their eyes have become benumed and tears steaming or rolling down their faces. It is undoubtedly the emotional separation of the human beings from a place which has played an active role of a family member and the same also witnessed their days of struggle, ordeal, construction,success,etc. After a short while they are on the street holding the bags on their shoulders. They have always preferred to carry even the heavy luggage to let any other person hold its tiresome weight.

Tripathi is smiling within himself as he is thankful to the college administration for inculcating in him and his fast friends the wisdoms of self effort, self reliance, self determination, self esteem, etc. For them, work is worship. It is the manifestation of their willpower/determination that they haven't hired any bullock cart or taxi to reach the railway station.

Raghunathpur is a well recognized town for its historical buildings, forts and temples. There is an enormous and enchanting temple of Lord Sri Ram which is on the way and is just before the hail of the town. That is all these friends conceive of this ongoing journey as a boon which has brought a pious opportunity to worship the almighty God. After performing their worship they eat prashad and drinks plentiful water from the sacred well of the temple premise. They reach the station in the noon ; they hear the the voice of the loudspeaker which reminds the passengers about the timely arrival of the train. Its exact arrival is at 2 P.M. and the clock rings an alarm which confirms the time of 1 o'clock. All the four friends decide not to waste their time in general gossips ; they advise Sajan to play Kishore Kumar's evergreen songs with the help of his mouthorgan and flute. The entire atmosphere of the station is eventually filled with positive energy and the fellow passengers bless him for his heroic skill of playing these musical instruments to create melodious voice which seems to be plunging deed into their inner souls.

The train has now arrived at the station and the passengers have started to board themselves in its respective compartment. Now the story takes a twist due to a large crowd of the passengers. A foreigner has just lost his Suitcase ; his face becomes pale due to sadness as he is a stranger to the place. Deepesh looks at him and tries his best to search the lost thing as he has never made any compromise with his humanitarian virtues and honesty. He finds the suitcase and happily hands over the same to its owner. The foreigner hails from South Africa and claps his hands by uttering the words 'Great country and great people'. He unbuttons his wallet and happily tries to give money to Deepesh but he refuses to accept it. The foreigner's great and pious words are enough and more precious than gold, diamond, money etc.

The train has now reached its destination and all these four friends promise one another to meet on the bank of the village pond during the evening time

4. Childhood Friend

**BHALLAM ANIL RAJU

'You don't have to meet him and convert the aversions worst from bad', the impudent order issued by Ramus' wife shall be breached and she knows it well.

Srinivas, childhood friend of Ramu visiting the Rangapuram village since he left 20 years ago. They had a great time as children when the villages were not under the verge of sharp political strifes. The people of power always invent a new attribute every time to divide people whenever their narrowness to enjoy incessant power thwarts them to be humane. Keeping in mind the ill-repercussions of meeting Srinivas in the present circumstances, Ramu limited himself to see his grown old friend after long gap and headed towards Srinivas house.

Srinivass' relatives were eagerly waiting for him outside of his house where he used to live. They are bi-hearting the sentences to utter for him to appease at the first meeting itself, a few owing to the hidden requests they had and other yielding to the middle-class obligation to be hospitable for a rich relative. To the surprise of the uneven roads of the village, a top brand luxurious car took turn to head towards the Srinivas house. Everybody excited as the car approaches, and a young man got off the car. He immediately overwhelmed by greetings and scripted sentences. Ramu has been observing all this by hiding himself behind a mango tree near to Srinivas house. Though he was excited to meet him, he couldn't dare for doing so.

20 Years back

Srinivas and Ramu were around 12 years old. Srinivass' father was the one of the foremost persons of the village who could receive education. He sold all the properties to establish a factory and was busy in rigorous arrangements for doing so. Srinivas despised the decision of his father and had no ear to listen him.

"We are leaving for Mumbai and I can't help it. I love this place and every other place without you would be a hell for me ", said Srinivas.

Ramu born to a poor handloom weaver who had to leave his studies soon owing to the wrecked financial status. His love for studies made him to look Srinivas situation as a great opportunity and said "No. You don't have to be sorrowful for that, actually it is an excellent opportunity for you to grow further. Don't think about me, we have been friends and we will be friend forever. You will get more like me. If I were in your situation, I wouldn't regret or think like this". Srinivas felt complacent with Ramus' remarks. They roamed on the roads as if the world ends on that day. They enumerated everything they have for them, from exchanging home-work books to stealing of mangoes from mango farms.

On the day when the fate decided to make two children apart, Srinivas and his family is waiting at the bus stop and were accompanied by their relatives who arrived to bid a farewell. The bus will arrive shortly and there is no sign of Ramu there. The bus arrived and everybody on board and about to start. Srinivas left his hope of meeting Ramu for the last time. But Ramu who is running hastily towards bus. Srinivas heart excited with Joy. Ramu handed over a hand-weaved shawl and said that till the shawl with Srinivas to think that he is with him.

It had been a week that Srinivas came to the village. He had been visited by the near by people of name and fame. It is expected for the only son of one of the top and influential industrialists in the country. Though Ramus mind oscillating between to have a volountary visit or to wait till he gets a call from Srinivas. The latter will be beneficial.

Under a peepal tree a group of children were playing, there the luxury car stopped.

Srinivas: Who is the child of Ramu here?

Radha: I am the daughter of Ramu. Who are you?

Srinivas: What is your name?

Radha: My name is Radha. But my father calls me Sri. By the by, who are you?

Srinivas: Why are you called 'Sri', when your actual name is Radha?

Radha: It my pet name and I am asking again that who are you?

Srinivas: Didn't you ask your father why do your father call you 'Sri'

Radha(infuriated): He calls me since my birth. You have been asking me all these and you didn't tell me who you are.

Srinivas (with a smile): Your uncle. Didn't your father tell me ever about me ?, I am his friend.

Radha: No. My father had a childhood friend and his name is 'Mangoes thief". You said you are my uncle, are you brother of my mother? because my mother said her brother was taken by God when he was at my age.

Srinivas: Yes. I am him.

Radha: Then, did God told you to go back?

Srinivas: Yes. God said " Your little niece is waiting, go and meet her'

Radha: It's not possible, my mom said, if anybody goes to God adobe, they will not come back.

Srinivas: I am an exception for that. Did you ever think about your uncle

Radha: Um. Many times. I always feel it wonderful if I had one to go visit him in holidays.

Srinivas: Yes. I am here for that. God here children. You go home and I am coming there.

Radha ran up in elation that she find her uncle and conveyed jubilantly about the arrival of her uncle. A bit of confusion between the couple of Ramu. First he suspected that its Srinivas and questioned Radha that was his name is Srinivas or mangoes thief. Radha replied none of the either and he is brother of her mother and God has sent him by listening her secret prayers.

The reply by Radha added more confusion. Dispelling that, Srinivas arrived at the house by walk in the narrow lane and appeared before the family. Radha yelled that he is her uncle sent back by God. Srinivas and Ramu stared each other for a minute. The entire childhood run through their minds. They hugged each other passionately and shed tears. The place acquired a sanctity due to the fragrance of their pure friendship.

They comfort themselves and sat down to ponder over all the days of childhood and after their break-up. Ramus' wife requested that he shall have dinner there on that night and she is going to prepare his favorite dish. Srinivas took Ramu to the favorite place of their childhood, a pond of lotuses edging God Sri Krishna Temple.

There at the Pond, they played like as they played in childhood. Sun started to sink in west. They tired by playing with stones, plucking lotuses, swimming etc. They sat on a bench facing each other and Srinu said that Ramu is no more living in the village and have to leave for Mumbai.

Ramu: Don't joke Mr. Mango Thief.

Srinivas: I am not joking. You listen it right. Your family is no more living in this sick village of politics and conundrums.

Ramu: The village is not sick. No village can be sick. You have got wrong information.

Srinivas: I am not a child my dear. I am not interested in any other activity here except meeting you. My father warned me to be cautious, and has told me the affrays between the castes, severe injuries made on the both the parties, imprisonments of a few, courts proceedings and bails etc. It took me one week to build the background to meet you. I had to meet every known and unknown, important and trivial to portray that I am here to meet everybody and nobody should comment nothing and create problem, especially for you and your family.

Ramu: These discrimination and fights are very common and takes birth before elections. These are too insignificant for one to bother. Just tell me how did you feel when you were honored with 'Young Industrialist Award'?. You made your father dreams realized and brought a grate fame to family.

Srinivas(irritated): We are not discussing about the awards and genealogies. Why are you taking these discriminations and affrays as very common things. When the politicians are so malevolent that they are sowing the poisonous seeds of enmity and ill-will in the innocent minds of people. They look innocence as the fertile ground ready to be sowed with terrible seeds of division. Utter useless to be here. Equality is a mirage here. No respect for a being as being. For people here cast is important to food. You are to leave this village immediately. I planned everything.

Ramu (deterministically): I born here; I die here. Mother earth gives everybody sustenance. The derailed human beings mind and thought would be set by herself.

Srinivas (Disgusted): Are you enjoying this man-made degenerative society and its catastrophic consequences and attributing solutions to the super natural powers?

Ramu: No. I am thoughtful and clear over the things. Soon, the court cases will be withdrawn. In 3 months, the annual celebration of village goddess takes place. For that the cooperation of all the communities is inevitable. The respective community heads meet up, they resolve the issues. And after a year or two, the village will be seeing a new conflict. It's endless. Human want peace if he is conflict, and vice versa. I beseech you not to ask me again to come with you.

Srinivas amazed at the wisdom and determination of Ramu. He thought it would be easy for him to take Ramu along with him. The defeated Srinivas, with heavy heart, requested Ramu to have at least accept a few currency notes and it was also rejected outright.

Srinivas was so happy at the uncompromising attitude of his best friend. Both of them went back to his home and had dinner together. Radha was so happy that he got her uncle. She asked Srinivas that if he has seen the God, how the God looks like, What sort of dress the God wears, etc., Srinivas took the opportunity to present ear rings to Radha. Srinivas put on them to Radha quickly so that Ramu couldn't have time to refuse the present.

Srinivas took a leave from Ramus family. Radha said she will visit Srinivas in her holidays. Ramu accompanied Srinivas to the end of the street and waits till the sound of car disappears.

Radha asked her father that when the god will sent her uncle again, Ramu passed for a while and replied "God vexed with your requests to have gold ear rings from your uncle, that's why God has sent him just for once. He already left our village. Waiting for him will be futile. He shall not come back. Sleep well". Radha dropped in slumber listening to the answer, without having much debate.

5. Strengthening the bond of Humanity in the wake of COVID-19

*****Dr. Rachna Rastogi***

Rudra Pratap works in a factory near Kharagpur and always puts his heart and soul to perform his assigned tasks up to the mark, with utmost devotion and commitment. His services were not impacted as the factory where he works comes under essential services and was rigorously working day in day out amidst the pandemic Covid-19.

On 20th April 2020, Rudra received a call from his family residing in Varanasi and came to know, that his 8 months son is detected Covid positive and later admitted to ICU, in a Hospital at Varanasi. The child suffered from severe diarrhea and high fever, followed by Covid, requiring immediate intense medical care.

way back in December 2019, soon after his marriage, Rudra in search of a better job shifted to Kharagpur with his wife. But destiny had kept some different plans for him. Just after two months of marriage Rudra lost his mother and the family had no one else other than his 78 years old father. Finding it extremely difficult to manage the situation without any support, Rudra decided to leave his wife Geeta in his parental home at Varanasi to look after his old father.

Time passed by, luck started smiling upon Rudra, he got promotion in his job from the post of a supervisor and became unit controller. Not only in profession, he was elevating but his family status also augmented as Rudra and Geeta got blessed with a baby boy. Rudra's reveries started growing leaps and bounds, instead of 8 hours Rudra started doing overtime in the factory to earn more money. Then came the first wave of Pandemic, Rudra was in Kharagpur and family was staying at Varanasi ,when it was declared complete lock down, inter-state movement was completely restricted. Transportation stopped, trains paused, no automobile movement was permitted, news and pictures of labor's migration were excruciating, and during such crisis situation Rudra, while working in factory received a frightful call from his wife telling about his newly born son falling sick. He was dying to immediately rush to his home to see his son but because it was a complete lock down situation, he was unable to find ways and means to reach home. Situation worsened after hospitalization of his son, also his father on exposure of hospital caught the Covid virus. Not only this, virus reached home making Geeta gruesome and down with fever and sore throat.

Stuck on duty and due to strict Covid-19 lockdown, it appeared to him next to impossible to reach home. His son's situation getting denigrated hour by hour. He literally screamed for help from authorities to save his son, he pleaded to cops, went to District magistrate office too to seek help, and was craving to see his son who saw the world for only 8 months. Geeta too was kept in isolation and was terribly crying out of the fear of losing her only son and begging doctors to see the glimpses of her infant and getting him the right treatment.

Rudra approached to the Cops at Kharagpur but due to stringent Covid regulation and banned interstate movement, nothing could be expedite. When Rudra was begging to the senior police officer and crying for assistance, there nearby was standing the apostle of God, happened to hear all the conversation between Rudra and the police. Seeing a father pleading for help and begging the permission to let him go to Varanasi, he called Rudra to the corner and instantaneously offered him the keys of his two wheeler to cover the distance by road from Kharagpur to Varanasi. Turns out, this fellow was nobody else than the Manager of the company where Rudra was working, who happened to come to the police station for launching the complaint of his lost mobile.

Culminating virus spread was a big challenge for the states that time, to preserve its people and restrict the commotion of people in the city, as covid cases were increasing alarmingly high. despite lockdown, yet on positive note, The Manager urged, higher authorities to give him the permission to cross state boundaries, considering family insurgency. He approached to the higher authorities and convinced them on humanitarian ground to help Rudra. Eventually "Go ahead" was given by Thana in-charge in consultation with Local District Authorities for rendering permission in his movement from kharagpur to Varanasi (UP), mentioning special conditions of travel amidst COVID-19 restrictions on humanitarian grounds. He also gave financial assistance to Rudra for immediate expenditure.

When going gets tougher, the tougher gets going in return. Rudra was constantly receiving calls from doctor indicating deteriorating condition of child. He immediate needs plasma cconvalescent therapy due to weakened immune system. Every single passing moment was raising the alarm as a threat to the life on the infant. Rudra drove the bike altogether 18 hours without a break and could manage to cross state territory uninterruptedly without any intrusion and reached Varansi. It took him some 19 hours to reach the spot. He then met the doctors and family, infant was experiencing chocked breathing and was unconsciously lying on bed, his body was not responding to any of the medication. Rudra hastily shifted his son to a different hospital equipped with better facilities. While shifting, there were hardly any sign of life, still Rudra didn't lose his hope and without caring his exhausted and acutely fatigued body due to excessive driving, Rudra arranged for ambulance and could get his child admitted for better treatment. Quick detection and prompt action could bring back the ray of hope onto the face of doctor, by inserting numerous medication and other necessary aids, doctors confirmed that life is still breathing inside the small body of the child.

Humanity and hope saved his son from "threat of life". Plasma therapy indicated affirmative response and child started sending recovering signals. That hard-hitting jiffy can be compared with the ray of sunshine that penetrates condensed woods and reaches to the topsoil and enriches fauna or like a desert to which, a drop of rain is not less than a drib of nectar. It was a heavenly moment for Rudra and Geeta, she too was shifted to the same hospital and through apt treatment and in particular the improving signs of infant bequeathed relief to her. But unfortunately Rudra's father could not be survived and destiny left an indelible imprint in the memory of Rudra and Geeta. The Happiness and satisfaction, which Rudra could witness was the result of exemplary act of humanity shown by the Manager who insisted and convinced the corps to assist him in crossing the state boundaries, not only this he assisted him by giving his vehicle and financial backing, because of which Rudra could reach Varanasi crossing 687.4 km via NH19. No religion is bigger than humanity and any adverse situation can be win over through the concord.

6. Childhood... "We Miss You"

****Dr. Mukta Goyal***

What was that childhood?
Brothers, Sisters, and Cousins all used to pull each other,
Used to tease and still live together,
We used to fight, fight, run, hold, laugh, cry,

Source:unsplash.com

Used to torment mother,
Papa used to come and give us the lesson of studies,
We used to hide in the quilt out of fear,
But whenever we used to pass,
No matter how many marks were there,
He also used to break coconuts.
Mother was perfect,
Neither yours nor mine,
Used to take care of everyone,
But did not think for herself,
That's my childhood, where are you?
We miss you, want to live it back,
Miss you. Miss you. Come Back.......... :)

7. Togetherness

** ***Dr. Jaya Ghosh***

Covid Today
Has made us come closer
Now that we are forced to stay indoors
To curb spreading
To be safe from invisible danger
And impending catastrophe.
It is sad to see
Even the devastating scenario around
Has not made people aware
It requires rules
To be imposed by the Government
To wear double masks
To use Sanitizers
To keep ourselves absolutely clean
To fight the new variants coming up from time to time
Ushering in pain, claiming innumerable lives
To streamline anxiety of human heart
For a brighter tomorrow.
Its time we realize the menace

And do the needful
Join our hands
And help in improving Community Health.

8. Success

Dr. Jaya Ghosh

The morning breeze seems to say
A new sun and a new day has come
With all its beauty and fragrance
New loves and new vistas untrodden.
That rouses in me
The thought that all is not lost
And at the end of the day
There would be a story
To savour sensuously.
Life is difficult at present
And everything seems to be dark all around
But we must keep our Hope
No matter what happens
Who might say what can make our day
An untold saga of a success story.

9. Journey Inwards

Dr. Jaya Ghosh

What a pity to see
That massacres have not also taught us to
Stop the stuff of mischief unlimited.
Revolutionless we are heading
Towards futility limitless.
It is time to look inwards
With increasing cases of forgery
What a pity to see
Several cheaters, liars, immoral people
Around us.

10. Work from Home

**By Dr Jyoti Patil

Home reminds us a cozy and carefree place,
Replenish our energies with stress-free space,
Where we rest and rejoice, with fun and ultimate choice,
Ignite our spirits, and fear not to raise our voice.
With the advent of COVID 19 as an invisible vulture,
Work from home as a part of corporate culture,
Seeped in and settled into our daily life,
Keeping social, nay physical distancing in rife.
Labelled with a beautiful name, CORONA our chief rival,
Lockdown and self-quarantine are only hope of survival,
Combating the invisible invader to escape infection,
Avoid contact with people to have a safe solution.
Remote Work Revolution 'work from home' they call it,
Not realising the repercussions a bit
Reaping benefits of that shift can accrue
Both to businesses and commuting time with no other clue.
Switching to shutdown mandate the only option,
For learning and joining office with precise precaution,

Zoom, Microsoft Teams, Slack, and Google Meet make us online,
Spending hours in video-conferencing, chatting cannot be fine.
But alas! Where is the peace we seek at home?
Belongingness and informal intimate dome,
'Home' promises us safety and security,
This makeshift office takes us towards gravity.
Keeping official environment intact,
Finding no place to rejoice and react,
No one at home are permitted to disturb,
Mental health is attacked with no cure or curb.
They say work should go on at any cost,
There is no better choice without any boast,
Office at home throws personal life at risk,
I think work from home is a bizarre mix.

11. New Normal Norms

***Dr Jyoti Patil**

A lot of firsts are happening these days
Thanks to this pandemic era,
Gone are the hay days, nothing pays,
When we go out, enjoy outings and opera.
At the beginning of the third decade of the Millennium,
In place of bringing happiness, peace, and prosperity,
It bringeth only fear and chaos, restricts life to the minimum,
Fear of death, fear of loss, fear of the virus, and fear of safety.
Living under the threat of constant changing mutants grown,
Enforced isolation, curtailed activities, celebrating no functions,
Fewer social connections and more time alone,
To stick to Sanitizer, social distancing, and masks with no options
With tremendous upheavals for all the inhabitants of the earth,
Effects of the pandemic as both acute and long-lasting,
Everyday family life changed, for many with no food, no hearth,
The deaths of loved ones and loss of jobs and forced fasting.
Grappling with post-pandemic's New Normal,
Man fears man, swirling societal frames,

Social intimacy and strong bonds turn formal,
'Tele-everything' and children with no outdoor games.
New normal dawns with negative repercussions,
The digital divide has broadened,
The technological change eliminates many jobs,
Economic inequality has worsened.
Accelerated adoption of digital technologies one has to cherish,
For work, school, and varied entertainment forms,
Switching to cashless transactions remotely to flourish,
And work from home as NEW NORMAL norms.

12. When To Stop Covid 19? Covid 2020/2021!!!!!!

****Dr. Devimeenakshi. K***

Unknown disease in universe
Unknown treatment for doctors
Unknown vaccination for scientists
Unknown side effects for all
Unknown types of viral infection
Unknown spread of diseases
Unknown reality during crisis
Unknown love from family members
Unknown house arrest for employees
Unknown disaster for many employers
Unknown predicament for labourers
Unknown bills of Government for pandemic
Unknown cause and effect for citizens
Unknown assumptions from media
Unknown of school education
Unknown results for college students
Unknown permanent reopening of institutions

Unknown fifty percentage of strength
Unknown opening for recreations
Unknown fact globally
Unknown unity in world
Unknown Prime Ministers/ Presidents on earth
Unknown agreements of countries
Unknown fourth wave
Yeh! Known future

13. Likes

***Dr. Devimeenakshi. K**

Everyone likes nature

Nature likes rain

Rain likes places

Places like people

People like money

Money likes boxes

Boxes like goods

Goods like spaces

Spaces like things

Things like quality

Quality likes durability

Durability likes longevity

Longevity likes history

History likes records

Records like events

Events like values

Values like virtues

Virtues like Merits

Merits like facts

Facts like evidence
Evidence like confirmations
Confirmations like permanency
Permanency likes stability
Stability likes firmness
Firmness likes decisiveness
Decisiveness likes Conclusiveness
Conclusiveness likes resolution
Resolution likes definition
Definition likes literature

14. Frailty

****Arundhati Dutta Choudhury***

We cannot look beyond....
Beyond the regime,
Beyond the red-blood pulsating life,
Or beyond the structural Faith,
Nothing and simply nothing...
The bearded grey man with void in his eyes,
The freshly blooming youth with dreams of many moons
Or the veiled shadows of human lives,
All gone to topless heaven or the bottomless hell
Because we could not look beyond the oldest shrine
And the echoing music of heaven.
Life becomes a deluge of faith, failing norms
As when, it disallows always to look beyond.

15. Citadel

***Arundhati Dutta Choudhury**

Upon varied loves and love alike
Is built the Citadel of life.
Fumes are lately seen,
Lately felt
And lately sighed,
And the Citadel stately grows to stand.
So evanescence were the days of the past.
So slightly ignored.
The seeming serious series of acts and facts
Have no steps to walk the Citadel-
Behind the bars, behind the burning pyre.
Today, leaning behind the rocky rhythmic slants,
I find the Citadel so firmly built,
Reflecting varied loves and love alike.
I sense the loss, the loss of evanescence fumes,
So deeply drive
Down the memory lane.
And reach the mountain fort,
My mighty Citadel where still

Memories brick the walls

And long-forgotten songs drape the casement case.

16. Dreaming of Hope

*****Arundhati Dutta Choudhury***

Cheering, flying wings
And a canvas of dust-doubt
Called hope,
Flaming the dying heat,
Damp, dislocated thoughts.
Un-relieving rest,
The lingering, measured moments of mind.
Often drowning deep, death-like,
Honesty is a priced gem,
A constant game parlour
Of living and un-living;
Of refusal and smeared signs of love.
The flying wings are carefree.
Free of charming hope,
The challenges to nothingness.
They are the charming cherubs of life,
Singing songs of everlasting faith,
When we toil and troll amid scores of
Moss dried uneven steps.

Leaving wishes behind,
Shuttling around the subtle coils,
The credentials of mortal life.

17. Chandeliers

***Arundhati Dutta Choudhury*

Drops of dripping pain,
Ribboned lines of curve and plain,
These are the graphs of life.
Bogus tales of bombastic lies,
Tales of laughing stock,
Tales of far away clouds
And misty minds,
All raspberry meadows
And broken blinds
Of series of Banquet Halls,
This is not life.
No life at all.
How playfully, they mask the chloroform scent.
Learn to love the false fragrance
Of care, love, and abundance.
These are the bells of my grand Chandelier.
The golden brooch of my henceforth life,
That remains forlorn before it burns.
Before it rocks behind the wind.

Or beside the rocking chair of pain.

18. Women

****Arundhati Dutta Choudhury***

In fumes and nauseated blood-red smell,
In the dark distance,
In the heaviness of masculinity,
In thumping footsteps,
Amid cries and corpses,
Stamps and guns,
Nocturnal antlers
Peep through shades and shelters;
Homes and huts....rearing bases....
Where a life progeny called
Women, girls, and females
Stay, grasp and carry
Their bodies all around.
In such roofless land
Women live to die
Because they are women—
Flesh only, pieces, chunks and
Later wounded bodily grudges.
We are highly high-necked,

Convict settled,
Quarantined.
Anytime to be snatched
To be etherized and dissected
By the Capuscular wolves
In distant hybrid lands.

19. School Days

****Rayba Saindane***

Let's be eccentric
Let's do something eccentric
Ask me anything
For it, my answer will be nothing
You will be asking I will be joking
Let's do something eccentric
We will do something different
For that, I will be ignorant
Be it abhorrent
Let's do something eccentric
We want to go to school
And we will land in the pool
On arriving on school ground
For late, let PT teacher will punish to make round
If we will make round, we will be sound
Let's do something eccentric
Let the kids', prayer be sung
While our tie topsy-turvy hang
On the class bench, we will bang

Let the class teacher take attendance
And we will have some steps of the dance
Let's do something eccentric
Let the English teacher teach,
Some words we will catch
And for fun tiffin, we will snatch
Let's do eccentric
When history teacher will come
We will do a sum
But what we read, let it be Mistry
We will ask him, his history
And madam's chemistry
Let's do eccentric
In computer, we will paint class
In commerce class, we will say alas!
Let's do eccentric

20. Mother

***Rayba Saindane**

Why you left me all alone mother...
Mother ...the dream you gave ...
Is to complete ...
You taught me to fly and fight
See your juvenile is yet to fight
Before your adieu
See your child's smile
See your child achieve mile
All happiness and luxury you eschew
To build the future of your juvenile
What not you did
A unique deed indeed
Did all sacrifice
To make this edifice
I saw you at hearth blew air through the pipe
But never let your child weep
I saw your work for me under the harsh sun
To feed your child bun
That harshness of the sun

indomitable spirit but never eschew
And could not stop You
To make me stand with elite
You turned all sorrow into delight
Some miles are achieved
Some are yet to be pursued
I saw poverty could not break you
For the sake of the child, considered all odds as few
how single penny you earned
To make me learned
I saw your struggles
Now these were the days
To reap your efforts' fruit
Before you pluck
In limitless silence, you stuck
Mother ...oh mother ...
Just see and listen to your children hark
Where shall I find you in this dark
You taught me etiquettes and manners
And to respect elders
And much more lessons
I'm left all alone with your teaching
Now I'm left all alone with your blessing
Mother o mother in this world no other divine
Mother With your legacy I stand alone
Your juvenile is yet to conquer
Why you leave me all alone mother

See your juvenile is yet to conquer
Your struggle is to bear fruit
Just a few days more wait...
Mother don't leave me all alone
Carve more lines of blessings on this Stone
Why you leave me all alone
Mother don't leave me all alone
It because you I live with ease
It is the not to cease
Because of you, I got everything
But to rear me you sacrificed everything
It was time to return something
Before you could get something
Why you separated
O dear departed
Why you leave me all alone mother
I'm to achieve something more
There is yet to conquer
O mother o mother.....

21. Quest

***Semanti Kumar*

I'll be the darkness to hail
Your Dawn.
To see your maddening smile,
I will be the Worries.
To weave your fabulous dreams,
I'll be the silent Night.
To make your wishes true,
I will be the shooting Stars.
But…..
Can you be the key
To unlock my Sky?

22. Alone

***Semanti Kumar

Remember that time cannot erase
The darkest scar that you made on my face.
The golden glory you already altered
To the dark and the filthy dirt.
Anytime anywhere
You could do many things for me…
But did you do any?
Don't remind me of your scary voice-
Over me and over my own choice.
Don't cut the roots of my dreams…
Cause they have their own and innate shine.
You tried to gag me in my breath
Now you have killed
All the purest faith.
You had brunt my hope with your own hand
And cast me off my lovely land.
Now, Can't you leave me alone?
I want to be the most Alone
In my world.

Then I shall lead,

I shall learn

I will find my own morn

I will see the skies

Through my own eyes.

23. Existing Today

***Semanti Kumar**

Don't expect truth
Just believe in lie.
Make yourself prove
If you want to fly.
Break your heart
But don't touch brain.
Lose support
Never feel any pain.
Live with yourself
Without any shame
Go ahead
Reject all kind of blame.

24. You

***Aashi*

Your words were
A soothing balm to my soul
The smile on your face
Was a ray of hope
For my infinite darkness
The burning fire in your gaze
Was the source of my salvation
Your ruby tinted lips
Shined like a sapphire stone
And covering the blank canvas
With hues and shades of red
It was your calming presence
Which brought me back from
The era of insanity
Warmth which was supposed
To be a foreign concept
Suddenly engulfed me
Bloomed chrysanthemums in my life
Swallowed my tears

Gave life a new beautiful meaning
Clouds breezed along the wind
Sun soared up
Birds chirped
People walked and talked
Until one day
Time halted itself for me
And you entered my life
So many memories to create
But such less time
What a shame
But nevertheless
I try
To live and love
Because this was the first lesson
You taught me
My love
Even if our souls
Are eons apart I will
Continue to love you
Unconditionally
Unconventionally
Wholeheartedly
You are the one for me
You are, you were and you will
Always be the one for me
Just like I am to you

So, fret not my love
You can close your eyes now
Do not worry about me
For I will follow you
One day
Get rest and rid yourself of the physical pain
Sorry for the times
You were alone
Not my intention
Not my way
Please forgive me
For not being able to do
Rid you of your pain
Even though you easily destroyed mine

25. You with me

*****Aashi***

You with me
Was pain
You with me
Was anger
You with me
Was betrayal
Once a safe haven
Now a network of coverts
You with me
Was supposed to be happily ever after
Not a strangled movie of core action
The vision was blindsided by you
Ears were echoing with your voice
The mind became an old projector
The heart hurts
Brain burns
Eyes once full of dreams
Turned ashen black with anger
Innocent endings

Turned into a vicious black tunnel
You with me
Is now a messy disaster
Don't know
What to feel
What to belief
Suffocation reigns at the highest level
Broken shards
Hurt the skin
You with me
Is waste
Hopes and dreams famished by you
Are illusions to capture
You are a good method actor
You with me
Turns out to be one single word
Life's lesson

26. Meet again

*****Aashi***

You left me
To wither and die
Took pleasure from my pain
I loved you with all my heart
Sacrificed everything
To be by your side
My happiness, my dreams
Wanting nothing but your love in return
You used me
And when I became useless for you
Dumped and destroyed me
My innocence shattered
Hatred infused
Not being able to get over shock
My soul rose again
Not with happiness but rage
Emotions shattered
But soul did not
From burning flames

Like a phoenix
I will come again
To destroy your world
Your happiness, your soul
You are going to
PAY and repent
You used me
Now I will use you
To come out on top
Darkness still surrounds me
But fear not
No matter how much I suffer
I will make sure
Your voice dies
The same way you killed mine
The same way you killed me
A day will come
When I will return the favour

27. Ember

*****Chethna Vivek N***

She once quoted:
"It is unsettling how some people
come close to you because of your warmth,
Then they light up a match and watch
you burn until your soul is in ashes
and all that remains are
little embers fading into dust.
And then they tell you it
was your fault all along."
To which he said:
"Then like a Phoenix you fly from the ashes.
I'll be the one to set you on fire.
See you fan the flames!! See you fly!!
Burning is an arduous part,
Just like the phase that both of us are in.
But we must cross it and if we did!
Trust me!!
It's Forever!! <3"

28. Pieces

***Nafisa Jhosawa**

The tiniest smiles were captured by the reflection in the colourless mirror.
The colossal presence emerged in the reflection,
supervising her efforts in the direction of
"PERFECTION."
The truth She had obscured as a result of a hundred different causes.
You can beat and roar, but she won't be heard.
You can beat and roar, but she won't bend.
His desire remained unfulfilled.
Aiming at targets, he chose to cheat.
Never once was he ready to accept defeat.
He simply chose the simplest way to mistreat every grain of wheat,
and finally decided to crush it completely.
But
the vulnerable grain kept returning to be crushed again and again.
The bond was like a ball that collided with a mirror

and shattered it to pieces.
And now I'm convinced that it accurately reflects my true self.

29. Nafisa Jhosawa

**Nafisa Jhosawa

Nafisa lives by the quote "if you have the courage to pursue your dreams, they will come true". A student of English, Psychology and Sociology, she is driven to help make an equitable society and contribute towards education.

Nafisa is an aspiring publisher, Writer as well as an Artist. She is actively writing a series of career handbooks which will encourage and inspire students to make an informed career decision. She entered the Independent Artists, Writers, and Performers forum to pursue her passions in research, experimenting, and discovering new skills with interest in humanistic studies.

30. The longing

*****Tenzin Tsetan***

Longing of the fresh air,
The ones I've never felt.
Caress of the sweet soil,
The ones I've never touched.
The uneven steps of roads,
Ones I have never seen.
My people on the other end,
that ignited hopes in each,
And to those I've never seen.
Glory to my motherland,
Glory to the martyred souls.
Year by year, the hope remains,
Sometimes dim but never out.
Watch us when we go back,
To the place we truly belong.
Watch us take our heart back,
The one that's rightfully ours.
Neck deep in the bloodied sea,
Karma comes for everyone.

And when it's time for you to face,
We'll be there to watch with grace.
Your foul face and ashen soul,
We pray no mercy for your sin,
But the conscious you deserted.

31. Women in Red

** ***Tenzin Tsetan***

The way of the universe,
Is it a blessing or a curse?
When it gives freedom to fly,
With the never-ending sky.
The world of opportunities,
Scoffed for its gender.
Wings of red that's cut and torn.
Sowing in, a rebel with the horns.
Moons and years of hushed tyranny,
Made her tears run cold and dark.
A wish, a desire, and a belief
In what she can show.
With the wings of knowledge,
And the stardust of chance.
The girl in red will soar up high,
Around the stars and equal to all.

32. One, Two, Three...

*****Venkatesan Sai Taruni***

One , two ,three, four , five , six , seven
There is a bird on the tree called raven,
Bright white cloth neatly woven
Sounds of the piano played by Beethoven.
Minds and actions reflected like a mirror
Life is a combination of thoughts like a stirrer,
Peaceful mind through meditation
Awful situation through hesitation.
Salute the the unconditional love of mother
There are many problems but do not bother,
Moral values given by father
Be cheerful and happy as we gather.

1.

33. Our Earth Has It's Garment...

****Venkatesan Sai Taruni***

Our earth has it's garment
It is the place of enjoyment,
Let's don't wait till the judgement
To save our beloved environment.
There are steep and high mountains
Filled with water like Fountains,
Fresh and green fields like lanterns
There are also white and spongy cottons.
The birds fly high in the sky
To make our day as vibrant as a dye,
What else do we need other the nature
Nothing, else but to save it's future.

34. The Carpenter Cuts The Wood…

*****Venkatesan Sai Taruni***

The carpenter cuts the wood
It is his livelihood,
Let's change our mood
To start doing good.
A plant grows as we sow as seed
Make way to help the need,
Let's accumulate some good deed
To avoid negative thoughts of greed.
Life is fully equipped with tools
We need to use them as per the rules,
Avoid being a fool
Try to cool.

35. Our Country is ...

****Venkatesan Sai Taruni***

Our Country is rich in poverty
When will we get the license of liberty?
If this prolongs there will be a calamity
With which everyone would lose their unity.
Look at the children filled with tears
We cannot do anything but act as viewers,
When will we there be a stop to these fears?
Will they take few more years?
Wake Up, Wake Up to end this pandemonium
To live with joy by playing harmonium,
Let's join our hands to show up our faces
So that our country would be in one of the peaceful places.

36. Here Comes The Charming…

****Venkatesan Sai Taruni***

Here comes the charming night
Oh! What a beautiful sight?
Filled with stars that give the light
Is it True? Am I right?
Oh My Dear elegant roses
Life is full of different phases,
Choose the right path for the races
So that you don't waste your chances.
Listen, Listen to the calm and soothing sound
Waves and Tides of the sea that surround,
People laughing at something that is found
But you don't involve, just travel around.

37. Here We Are Sitting…

***Venkatesan Sai Taruni**

Here we are sitting infront of the laptop
There farmers harvest the crop,
The children playing as they hop
Maiden working and cleaning with mop.
Milk and cheese from the dairy
Blessings from our beloved fairy,
Avoid being bored and slothy
Make your life worthy.
This is the new month called June
Make it charming as it is a boon,
Try to reach the moon
As the time passes soon.

38. A Red tale

****Shrishti Kothari***

It was fifteenth of November,
The naive teenager Shrishti got a reminder.
She woke up to a stain on her bed
and a transforming reminder.
In India, It's also a reminder for some families
to host a traditional party, when a girl attains puberty.
But the family she grew up in, had no such ritual,
yet the situation didn't seem casual.
She rushed into the loo
With a change, she never went through.
She then realized it was her "First Period"
For which she was ready not yet.
Her eyes were flooding with tears.
Tears of sorrow with a feeling of,
"Ugh, but why am I crying?" and laughs.
Shrishti was now in the squad of big girls.
She stood stiff with her stomach cramps and
Pledged, "I now take intervention
From making jokes on menstruation. Period.

Shrishti was now in the squad of big girls.

Author's Bio

Disha Madan

Dr Disha Madan is teaching at the Department of Studies in English at Nehru College & PG Centre, Hubli (Karnataka). She is a creative writing specialist, a social activist, and has published books on American Women Writers and Cultural Studies. She publishes a bi-annual research journal "Impression" for budding research scholars. Recently she has published a novella, ' Crossing Over '.

A well known social figure in the twin cities of Hubli-Dharwad , she was the President of Innerwheel Club of Hubli Mid-Town, IIW Dist 317, for the year 2015-16.

[1]P. V. B.Sriramamurthy

[1]Sri PVB Srirammurty is well qualified, and a very reputed, versatile Telugu short story writer. Having begun to write stories at the age of 15, he

has written more than 350 stories and 10 novels. They were published in different weekly and monthly magazines. He has penned many spiritual essays in The Eenadu a famous Telugu daily in Andhra Pradesh.

He has given many talks on the radio. He has also written 10 radio plays. Has reviewed many books, written forewords, and acted as a judge for short competitions. Many awards wedded this highly talented writer. Has been felicitated on many occasions. He is adept at using the dialect of his district in the right proportion. Being the resident of Vizianagaram, he leads a peaceful retired life Satisfactorily. He still writes stories.

[2]Dr Karunanidhi Ketireddy.

[2]Dr Karunanidhi Ketireddy is currently working as Head of the Department/Course Coordinator for the Department of Commerce and Management Studies in Dr B. R. Ambedkar University, Etcherla, Srikakulam, Andhra Pradesh State, India. He is a member of the board of studies for Management Studies. Dr Karunanidhi is a popular columnist for Eenadu Newspaper which is a daily newspaper in the regional language of Andhra Pradesh. He wrote books on Cashew Industry and his works were also published as chapters in several books. He attended several international and national seminars and published his research writings in Scopus journals. Dr Karunanidhi rendered his services as Project Director for Centre for Training Research and Development an NGO based at Vizianagaram. He is a member of WELLTTE. He is serving as a member of evaluation for MBA and MCOM Viva voce for JNTU and several other universities of Andhra Pradesh State. Dr Karunanidhi is a creative social worker who started the Gift a Plant program in Srikakulam District and distributed hundreds of saplings on birthday events and ask them to grow the plant. … … …

Dr. Alok Chandra

Dr. Alok Chandra is an Editor, Poet, Author, Critic who hails from Bargaon, Nalanda, Bihar. He is the Vice -President of World English Language Learners, Teachers and Trainers Association (WELLTA) - Bihar.

He is the Editor/Editorial Board Member of three renowned international peer reviewed and referred journals, Journal of English Language and Literature (JOELL), The Creative Launcher, The Expression. He is the former research scholar of the Dept. of English, Nava Nalanda Mahavihara, Deemed to be University, Under Ministry of Culture, Govt. of India, Nalanda, Bihar.

He has participated and presented his papers on diverse fields of English literature in national and international conferences/ seminars ; he has got his numerous research papers published in both international peer reviewed journals and edited books. He possesses an expertise in ecocriticism/ecocritical theories. His poems have got published in reputed journals and anthologies.

He is the recipient of best research paper award in a national conference for his eco-sensitive paper entitled "The Poetry of Gary Snyder : An Ecological Perspective", organized by the Dept. of English, Andhra Loyola Institute of Engineering and Technology, Vijayawada, Andhra Pradesh.

So far, he has got published his four edited books entitled "Revisiting Ecology, Culture, Myth, Gender and Diaspora in Literature", "Shades of Floating Muses"(An Anthology of Poems), Phenomenal Voices : An Anthology of Short Stories", and "Perspective on Ecocriticsm in Contemporary Literature".

Bhallam Anil Raju

Bhallam Anil Raju is a poet, story writer and a lecturer of Physics and Mathematics who hails from Marlapalem Village of Andhra Pradesh State (PIN-521214). He has profound interest in pursuing the studies in Physical Sciences, Mathematical Sciences, English Literature and ancient Indian philosophical texts. He has been inspired, guided and monitored by Prof. Kotari Surya Chandra Sekhar, HOD, English Department, Sir CRR Degree College, Eluru, Andhra Pradesh (PIN-534007). He worked as Physics lecturer and as a Postman in Postal Department. He is currently working as Librarian for Kendriya Vidyalaya Tamenglong-Manipur, KVS, Ministry of Education. Government Of India.

Dr. Rachna Rastogi

Dr. Rachna Rastogi is a former Professor, Dean Student Affairs & SM Club Coordinator, at GLA University Mathura & Gsfc University, Vadodara. Dr. Rachna is also a Freelance Writer, Corporate-Trainer, Poet and Social activist. She had been the Bio-Farma, Elsevier journal reviewer for Language. Dr. Rastogi is a Certified Trainer for Human Values and Professional Ethics form IIT Kanpur did her P.hD. in 2003 from Ruhilkhand University, has attended various short term courses on Soft Skills form IIT Roorkee, & Kanpur and has to her credit various research papers & poems published in journals and chapters in proceedings and books.

Consecutively for the year 2018 and 2019 Dr. Rastogi has been awarded as best faculty coordinator by IIT Mumbai, Powai, during Tech-radiance.

Dr. Rachna Rastogi has delivered various lectures for corporate trainees like GATL, GIPCL, GSFC Ltd. etc. and has organized 6 weeks long substantial and innovative Foundation Course for B.Tech, MBA and BSc students giving exposure of potential life skills programs i.e. Narcotics Prevention, First Aid, Road Safety, Digital interface, Health and Hygiene, Corporate Ethics etc., in association with eminent faculties form IITs and Government organizations at GSFC University. She has also actively organized a substantial Swachhta drive in and around Vadodara in association with VMC, under the guidance of Mr.P K Taneja, IAS (Rets.) (Former Additional Chief Secretary to Govt. of Gujarat. Dr. Rachna Rastogi has also actively carried the interface between Industry and academia to facilitate value teaching and hands on learning experience for Science, Engineering and Management aspirants.

Dr. Mukta Goyal

Dr Mukta Goyal is a dedicated professional having an experience of almost a decade in academia. Presently she is working as a Principal in Manvi Institute of Edu. &Tech, Delhi, SCERT. She has completed her Ph. D. in Management from Mewar University, Chittorgarh. She has been conferred with the "Best Principal "Award in the year 2022 along with “The Real Super Woman" Award in the year 2020. She holds her credit to author four books and also edited around Twenty books with different titles. She is also a regular columnist in newspapers and very much acclaimed for her poetries. Many of her research papers have been acknowledged and published in the Journal of National and International repute as well as conference proceedings too.

Dr. Jaya Ghosh:

Dr. Jaya Ghosh, presently working as Assistant Professor, The Department of English, Dr. Gour Mohan Roy College, Monteswar, Dist. : Purba Bardhaman, PIN : 713145, W.B. has participated and presented papers in several State/National level Seminars and International Conferences. She has also published articles on various literary disciplines.

Dr. Jyoti Patil

Dr Jyoti Patil professionally holds an administrative post of a principal in a local college in Nagpur with 33 years of teaching experience. Basically, she is poet at heart and a creative writer by passion. Her poems and stories have been published in various magazines, books, journals and national dailies. She has also published an anthology of her poems titled *Living beyond Life* (2018) composed mostly on nature and life. She has received Golden Book of Records' recognition for her poems on Corona in 2020 appeared in GEM III.

Dr. Devimeenakshi. K

Dr. Devimeenakshi.K is an Assistant Professor (Senior) in English Department of School of Social Sciences and Languages, Vellore Institute of Technology, Chennai. Her specialisation is on English Language Teaching (ELT), and did her Ph.D. in ESL and EFL, and a trainer of Soft Skills Training. She published Scopus-Indexed papers, papers in International Research Journal of Social Sciences and Humanities, even published trans/multi-disciplinary article in Scopus-Indexed journal with impact factor. Moreover, she worked on students' mini projects as guide. Her publication with foreign professor, later, invited him as an Adjunct Professor for University is remarkable. Attending/conducting workshops, presenting papers in International Conferences, and delivering/ organising guest lectures are some feathers in her cap. She was BEC coordinator and coordinator of Toastmasters International Club, VIT Student Club/Chapter. She is now faculty coordinator for English Literary Association, Chennai, and recently conducted a Workshop along with Rotary Club of Temple City, Chennai. She has reviewed a few research papers for SCIENCEDOMAIN International Publishing Group. She is an ardent and sincere researcher as well as teacher in English language teaching.

Arundhati Dutta Choudhury

Arundhati Dutta Choudhury is an Associate Professor, in the English department of Radhamadhab College, Silchar. Her Area of

Specialization is American Literature, Commonwealth Literature, and Ecofeminism.

Career Objectives & Self Interest: An inclination to complete Ph.D. and to undertake a Research Project as part of Career Advancement Process.

Further studies in Commonwealth literature and a future provision to enlarge the interest into post-doctoral research. Creative writings regarding pertinent social issues and female predicament to be criticized and interpreted.

Rayba Saindane

Raiba Saindane is a teacher of English and social science who hails from Jalgaon, Maharashtra. He is presently teaching in SDJ international school, Surat, Gujarat.
He is an M.A. in English and has cleared NET/SET in English literature.

Semanti Kumar

She is presently a student of English Honours in Hooghly Mohsin College, West Bengal. She is highly interested in Writing, Painting and Gardening. Some of her poems and stories are published in renowned magazines like KURI KOROK, KICHUKHHON, HOICHOI (IOWA, USA). She did her additional course in Content writing. Her goal is to be creative as well as an independent and good citizen.

Aashi

Aashi Prasad is currently pursuing her Master degree from Jyoti Nivas College (Autonomous), Bengaluru.

Chethna Vivek N

Chethna Vivek is currently pursuing her UG degree from Jyoti Nivas College (Autonomous), Bengaluru.

Nafisa Jhosawa

Nafisa Jhosawa is currently pursuing her UG degree from Jyoti Nivas College (Autonomous), Bengaluru.

Tenzin Tsetan(Jyoti Nivas college Autonomous ,Bangalore)

She is a Tenzin and a Tibetan. Raised up in the south, She always enjoyed reading.She didn't have a phone till I reached 10th standard. So, to spend the hours not wanting to study, She would dive into all sorts of fiction novels and soon She found herself spending every penny She had on books and her parents were very supportive of it. After a while,She wrote poems so as to show her emotions without letting anyone know, realising that She had a nag for it, She started writing more and more. Be it on life, loss or even freedom, it gave her a sense of comfort and a longing that if people were to read it, maybe they'll understand that they are not alone. From a 21 year old to anyone who loves reading, She hope you find your peace in your own self.

Venkatesan Sai Taruni

Venkatesan Sai Taruni is a student in St. Francis College For Women, Hyderabad, Telangana pursuing BA (Economics, Political Science and Public Administration). She began writing poems at the age of 17. Her poems include diversified themes and perspectives on various topics. She likes poetry, reading books(philosophy) and music.

Shrishti Kothari

Shrishti Kothari is currently pursuing her UG degree from Jyoti Nivas College (Autonomous), Bengaluru.

9 798887 041346

Printed by Libri Plureos GmbH in Hamburg,
Germany